Key stage 3

Oxford

Black peoples *of the* Americas

NIGEL SMITH

Contents

Oxford University Press

OXFORD
UNIVERSITY PRESS

Great Clarendon Street,
Oxford OX2 6DP

Oxford University Press is a
department of the University of
Oxford. It furthers the University's
objective of excellence in research,
scholarship, and education by
publishing worldwide in

Oxford New York
Auckland Bangkok Buenos Aires
Cape Town Chennai Dar es Salaam
Delhi Hong Kong Istanbul Karachi
Kolkata Kuala Lumpur Madrid
Melbourne Mexico City Mumbai
Nairobi São Paulo Shanghai
Taipei Tokyo Toronto

Oxford is a registered trade mark of
Oxford University Press
in the UK and in certain other
countries

© Oxford University Press 1992
First published 1992
18 17 16 15 14 13 12

ISBN 0 19 917201 3

Typeset by MS Filmsetting
Limited, Frome, Somerset
Printed in Hong Kong

Preface

This book examines the history of black people
in the Americas through an investigation into
the two central questions set out in chapter I.

- How have black people been treated in the
  Americas?
- How has the experience of black people
  affected the course of American history?

Having established these questions, pupils have
the opportunity to form initial hypotheses
before examining a variety of evidence to help
them reach their final conclusions. Key
questions are set out in each chapter which
relate directly to the two central questions. At
the end of each chapter pupils should reflect on
how the content of that chapter helps them to
test their initial hypotheses.

After the first introductory chapter the book is
organised chronologically and more than
encompasses the content demands of the
National Curriculum. The study of slavery and
of its legacy are essential in trying to
understand American history and society.
Studying this topic will also assist pupils to put
into perspective and understand many
controversial issues involving 'race' and colour.
Teachers will find a great deal in this book to
stimulate discussion and further work on a
range of topics. Many links exist between the
subject matter of this book and the content of
other study units.

Nigel Smith

Notes to teachers

Exercises offering opportunities for developing
pupils' understanding of concepts and skills
are signposted as follows:

Changes 17 35 38 47
Causes and Consequences 9 13 17 24
30 34 45
People in the Past 23 27 29 31 35 39
42 43
Different Views 37
Evidence 11 15 19 25 33 41 46

Black Americans

You may have laughed at a joke that poked fun at someone because of their race or nationality. You may have heard people insulting others because of the colour of their skin or the country they come from. You may have heard people talking about racial prejudice. Racial prejudice is the belief that one group of people is superior and better than those of a different colour or 'race'.

These words were written in 1963 by Dr Martin Luther King, a black American leader:

You suddenly find your tongue twisted and your speech stammering as you seek to explain to your six-year-old daughter why she can't go to the public amusement park that has just been advertised on television, and see tears welling up in her little eyes when she is told that 'Funtown' is closed to colored children ... a five-year-old son asking: 'Daddy, why do white people treat colored people so mean?'.

(Martin Luther King, letter from Birmingham City Jail, 1963)

Martin Luther King

Many times in history one group of people has dominated and persecuted another group. Sometimes people living in the same country fight one another because they are a different colour,

speak a different language or worship God in a different way. There are countries where conflicts like this are going on at the present time. Some of the worst cases of man's inhumanity to man have been when one 'race' of people has shown prejudice* and intolerance to another.

This book is about the way in which a minority of people in the United States of America, black people, have been treated by the white majority. It is also about the struggle of black Americans against the prejudice they have suffered to take their place as equals alongside every other American. By learning how black people came to be in the Americas in the first place, we can try to give an answer to that question asked by the five-year-old child: 'Why do white people treat colored people so mean?'

The USA has always suffered from divisions between white and black Americans. Many times white people have stopped black people from being equal citizens. In this 1960 photograph a black American meets opposition from a white American.

Black people of the USA are the nation's second largest racial group. 'Black people are really just like everybody else. Some of them are exceptional and most of them are not.'

(Black writer James Baldwin)

* PREJUDICE

To dislike someone or something without any good reason.

In 1492 when Columbus reached the Americas, he thought he was in the East Indies and so he called the natives 'Indians'. White people often call them 'Red Indians' but they should really be described as Native Americans.

⊞ The USA

America is made up of people from many different countries and races. There are about 250 million people living in the United States of America. Most of them are white but nearly thirty million, or one in eight, are black. Four hundred and fifty years ago there were only a few white people and virtually no black people at all. The first native Americans were the so-called Indians. There were probably about three million Indians at the time the first white immigrants* began to arrive.

Starting in the seventeenth century some Europeans from England, Spain and Holland made the difficult journey across the Atlantic Ocean to build settlements in what they called the 'New World'. Some of them, such as the Pilgrim Fathers, were seeking greater freedom to worship God as they wished. Others saw America as an opportunity to own their own land, work on their own farms and build a better life for their families than was possible in their home country. Many of these new Americans disliked the governments in Europe where people had few political or religious freedoms. Europeans were not able to vote or choose who governed their countries. Many of them had to practise religion in the way they were told to by their king or government. Land in

The black population of the USA: 1790–1990

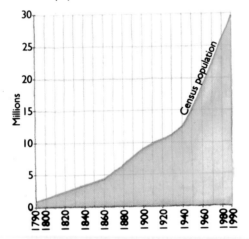

Percentage of black population by region: 1988

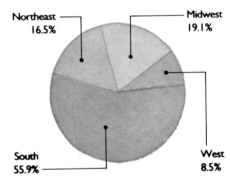

Most black Americans live in the southern part of the USA

Regions of the USA

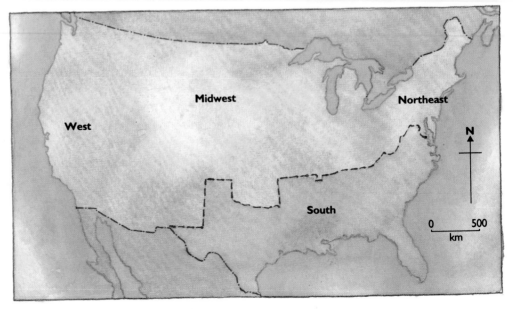

Europe was owned by a fairly small class of aristocratic land-owners. Most people who worked on the land remained poor throughout their lives.

Gradually the Americans living in the thirteen British colonies began to dislike British control and taxation. In 1776 they rebelled and declared their independence from the king and government of Britain. This is what they said in their 'Declaration of Independence' which set up the USA: 'all men are created equal' with the right to 'life, liberty and the pursuit of happiness'.

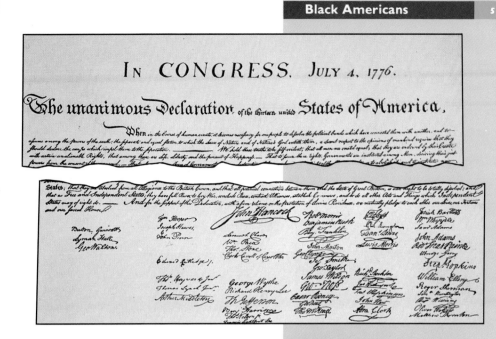

Photograph of the Declaration of Independence

DECLARATION OF INDEPENDENCE

1 What do you think the words quoted from the Declaration mean?

2 Why do you think Americans believed these ideas were important?

Even with the creation of the USA founded on these ideals, one important group was deliberately left out of any share in the freedom and opportunity that was offered. The fine promise of 'liberty' did not apply to the black people living in the United States. Even George Washington, first President of the USA, saw no contradiction or anything wrong in his keeping black people as slaves.

▤ The African past

White people thought that Africans were inferior and uncivilised. This idea justified the discrimination and exploitation of black people. In fact there were important kingdoms and great civilisations* in Africa at the same time as people in Britain were living in primitive iron-age huts. From Egypt, an African country, came ideas about geometry, arithmetic and astronomy. The pyramids, one of the seven wonders of the world, are a reminder to us of the skills and power of ancient Egyptians. West Africa too had a long-established civilisation.

Religion and the family were very important to Africans. But white people could not understand the value and importance of religions that were not Christian. Africans valued the idea of the family more than most Europeans did. The old, the sick and the disabled were always taken care of within the family. Whites sometimes claimed that tribal wars were evidence that Africans were uncivilised. Many of the wars were not really that serious and it is thought few people were killed. The most destructive wars in our world have been fought by white nations.

* CIVILISATION

A well-developed and orderly society.

This sixteenth-century bronze plaque from Benin in West Africa shows a king, known as an Oba, with two chiefs. The arrival of the European slave-traders destroyed this great civilisation.

THE AFRICAN PAST

1 What evidence do we have that Africans were civilised?

2 Why do you think white people thought that Africans were uncivilised?

The different reasons why people went to live in America

Africans went to live in America for quite different reasons from the white settlers. These black people were forcibly taken from their native land. They had no choice where they lived or where they worked. They were prisoners of the dreadful system of slavery* that put them entirely at the mercy of white Americans. The Americans did not invent slavery. Slavery had existed in Africa for thousands of years. In Europe the great Roman Empire had depended on millions of slaves. From the fifteenth century many other countries in the Americas had slavery, as you can see from the map. Many black British people are descendants of the slaves who lived in the Caribbean islands, such as Jamaica and Barbados.

The main countries importing slaves: 1451–1870 (imports in thousands). Slaves were imported into South America in large quantities as well as North America and the Caribbean.

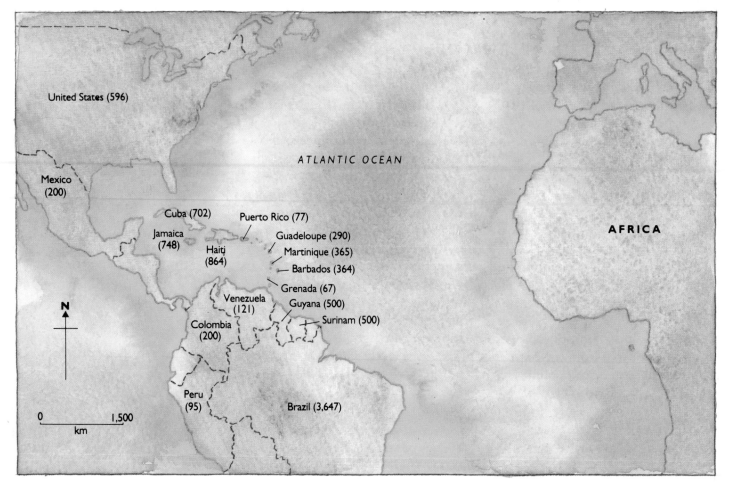

The black experience

Slavery had a powerful impact on the development of the USA. Sooner or later a nation founded on the principle of liberty was bound to argue over slavery. As you will discover, it took a major war to finally end slavery. But even after slavery was abolished and the former slaves were freed, black people did not gain equal rights or opportunities. Many white people continue to look down on them and to discriminate against them. The fact that they are black makes them easily identifiable. Today many black Americans are very much aware of how black people came to be in America in the first place. They know of the suffering and struggles of members of their families during the past three hundred years. Perhaps some of them feel bitter at the past and sometimes present treatment of black people in the USA. Often the experience of black people has been that they have been treated in their own country as if they were not Americans at all.

Your investigation

A hypothesis is a theory or explanation of historical events that we can test against evidence to find out whether or not it is right. In this book you will be investigating two main questions:

How have black people been treated in the Americas?
How has the experience of black people affected the course of American history?

Use the material in this chapter, and your own ideas, to form initial hypotheses to answer these questions. As you work through the rest of the book, use the evidence to test your hypotheses, before coming to final conclusions.

As historians it is important that we use the correct words and terms. Different words have been used to describe black Americans. For a long time they were referred to as negroes and often, to insult them, the word 'nigger' was used. Many whites called them 'coloured people'. Since the 1960s the term 'black' has become normal, although some people prefer the term 'Afro-American' as a reminder of their original roots in Africa. In this book I have used the terms 'black' or 'black American' although in some of the documents other expressions may crop up.

The story in this book is not a pleasant one. There are many inspiring accounts by people who fought against injustice. But there are also many sad accounts of people who suffered. You must remember that everything in this book is about real people, black or white, like ourselves, with hopes and fears about their lives. By studying the history of what happened to these people we may be better able to recognise persecution, racial discrimination and injustice where it exists in our world today.

The first 'stars and stripes' flag in 1776 was a symbol of freedom for a new nation that still permitted the keeping of black people as slaves. This picture shows the flag flying on the home of Betsy Ross, who made the first flag in 1776.

SLAVE

A person who is owned by another person.

From freedom to slavery: the slave trade

● *What was it like to be taken by force to be a slave?*
● *How did slavery affect the way that black and white people thought of each other?*

It is very hard for us to imagine what it was like to be taken by force from Africa to America as a slave. Never again did the slaves see their families or their native land. Instead they were made to work long hours for their 'master'. Many were treated cruelly because they had no rights as slaves. Millions of Africans suffered this treatment under the dreadful system of slavery. You might well find it difficult to understand how such a cruel system could be allowed to flourish.

One reason was that British ship-owners and sailors made large sums of money out of slavery and English ports such as Bristol and Liverpool prospered as a result. This is how the slave trade operated. There were three stages:

First stage

Ships left a British port loaded with goods made in England, such as tools and weapons, that were wanted in Africa. Crews with guns went ashore and captured any young blacks they met. Some local African rulers captured blacks from other areas and sold them to the slave-traders. They were afraid that if they didn't they might be captured and sold themselves. On the west coast of Africa the goods would be exchanged for Africans kidnapped inland.

Second stage

This dreadful part of the ships' journey was known as the 'middle passage'. The ships, now packed with Africans chained to one another below decks, sailed two and a half thousand miles across the Atlantic Ocean to America. The journey took from eight to ten weeks. Some of the Africans were so desperate they tried to jump overboard or kill themselves by refusing to eat. Sometimes a crew member would break their teeth and force food into them. Loss of a slave's life was a loss of money for the sailors.

Third stage

The Africans would be sold in the Americas to be slave labourers. The ships' captains would use the money from their sale to buy a third cargo of sugar, spices or tobacco. They sold this for a further large profit in England.

This early etching shows Africans being chained on board a slave ship.

At each stage large profits were made and ships' captains and crews gained considerable fortunes out of the slave trade. Some captains used a system called 'loose packing' to deliver slaves. Under that system, captains took on board fewer slaves than their ships could carry. They hoped to reduce sickness and death among the slaves. Other captains preferred tight packing. They believed that many blacks would die on the voyage anyway and so carried as many slaves as their ships could hold. Captain Collingwood of the Liverpool slave ship *The Zong* threw 132 slaves overboard. He thought the insurance money would be worth more than sick slaves. He was never tried for murder.

A poster advertising a slave sale.

TO BE SOLD, on board the Ship *Bance-Island*, on tuesday the 6th of *May* next, at *Ashley-Ferry*; a choice cargo of about 250 fine healthy NEGROES, just arrived from the Windward & Rice Coast. —The utmost care has already been taken, and shall be continued, to keep them free from the least danger of being infected with the SMALL-POX, no boat having been on board, and all other communication with people from *Charles-Town* prevented. *Austin, Laurens, & Appleby.*

N. B. Full one Half of the above Negroes have had the SMALL-POX in their own Country.

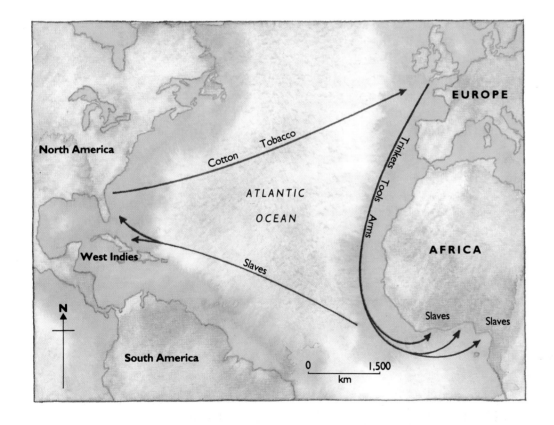

The slave trade triangular route

Sir John Hawkins was a successful English slave-trader in the sixteenth century. He designed this crest for himself.

THE SLAVE TRADE

1 Why were so many slaves packed on to the ships?
2 What words can you think of to describe the conditions on the slave ships?
3 Why was the 'triangular trade' so profitable?
4 What is your opinion of the owners and crews of the slave ships?

≋ Conditions on the ships

How do we know what this trade was really like? We can read the evidence of some of those who witnessed it. Here are the views of some of the slave-traders themselves.

Source A

'The sights I witnessed may I never look on such again', wrote the captain of a slave ship after his first voyage. 'This is a dreadful trade.'

(An English captain in the eighteenth century)

Source B

They had not so much room as a man in his coffin, either in length or breadth. It was impossible for them to turn or shift with any degree of ease.

(A captain describing conditions below decks during the 'middle passage')

But only somebody who had actually been kept in those conditions could really know the horror of such a journey. Gustavus Vassa was kidnapped at the age of eleven from his family and sold into slavery. He was a real person and this is part of his personal account of being taken by ship to America:

Source C

The complexions of the crew were different from mine and so was their long hair and the language they spoke. I thought I would be eaten by those white men with horrible looks, red faces and long hair. I now saw that I would have no chance of returning to my native country. Under the decks the smell was loathsome. I wished I were dead. When I did not eat they held me fast by the hands and flogged me severely. The crew watched us closely in case we leapt into the water.

I was told we were to be carried to these white people's country to work for them. The white people acted in such a savage manner and I had never seen such brutal cruelty. The shrieks of the women and the groans of the dying made it a scene of horror. One day when we had a smooth sea and a moderate wind two of my countrymen who were chained together, preferring death to a life of misery, jumped into the sea.

(*The Interesting Narrative of Gustavus Vassa,* 1791)

In the seventeenth century the pace of the slave trade quickened. Large areas of North America were being settled and English colonies were established along the east coast. The West Indies in the Caribbean were also settled by the English. The Portuguese and Spanish began to take over South America. All these Europeans wanted to use slaves in their new colonies. Between 1698 and 1807 an average of one slave ship left a British port every two weeks. After collecting slaves in Africa they sailed on to America. The table on the right shows the official figures for 1771.

This diagram shows how the slaves would be packed tightly below the decks of a slave ship. The large section on the right contains 124 men slaves, the next 58 boys, the next section has 83 women and the small room in the stern has 27 young girls. Sometimes they would be taken up in batches to exercise and get some fresh air on deck.

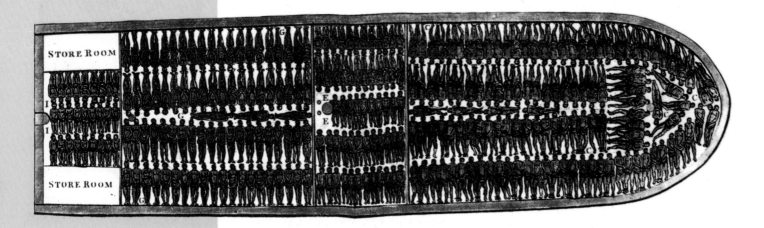

STORE ROOM

STORE ROOM

Probably about twenty million Africans were taken against their will to North and South America. We will never know how many millions more died during their capture or on the slave ships. Finally in 1807 Parliament put a stop to British ships taking part in the slave trade. The USA followed in 1809, France in 1815, and the Spanish and Portuguese in 1820. But although no new slaves could be taken from Africa, slavery in the Americas continued for many more years.

Some English people were appalled by this trade but it was left to a religious group, The Quakers, to start a campaign against it. In 1787 a committee was set up to oppose the slave trade. One member, Thomas Clarkson, visited Bristol and Liverpool to talk to the sailors who worked on the slave ships. His book, *A Summary View of the Slave Trade*, did a great deal to expose the evils of the slave trade.

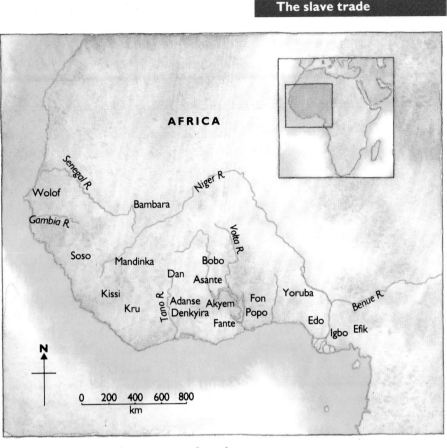

The main peoples who were used as slaves
The slave trade did great damage to the way of life of many African tribes. It also poisoned relations between black and white people.

From **Liverpool** 107 ships sailed that carried 29,250 slaves (*Africa–America*)
From **London** 58 ships sailed that carried 8,136 slaves (*Africa–America*)
From **Bristol** 23 ships sailed that carried 8,810 slaves (*Africa–America*)
From **Lancaster** 4 ships sailed that carried 950 slaves (*Africa–America*)
(The number of slave ships leaving England in 1771)

EVIDENCE: WHAT WERE CONDITIONS DURING THE MIDDLE PASSAGE REALLY LIKE?

1 What did Gustavus think of the appearance of the crew?
2 What was his opinion on the behaviour of the white people?
3 Why do you think he would not eat?
4 Why were the slaves kept chained together?
5 What do you think would have been the worst part of such a journey?
6 Why are Sources A, B and C useful to historians?
7 Which of these sources and illustrations is most useful for historians investigating conditions on slave ships?
8 How reliable are Sources B and C?
9 Why do you think the captains in Sources A and B continued in the slave trade for another twenty years?
10 Write extracts that might have appeared in the log book* of a slave ship describing the three stages of the ship's journey.

* **LOG BOOK**

A book in which the details of a journey are kept.

*

INFERIOR

A person who is not considered to be as good as or equal to others.

≋ The reasons for slavery

Settlers in America wanted slaves. They could force slaves to work for long hours in the fields and of course they were cheaper than white labour. In 1793 Eli Whitney made his simple new machine for separating cotton fuzz from the cotton seeds, and cotton became the great crop of the southern part of North America. As cotton became more important so did slavery. There was a shortage of white labourers. Africans, so it was argued, were used to the extreme heat that is normal in the south of the USA. In addition, some slaves gave birth to new slaves which was an extra bonus for the slave-owners. Sometimes the owner himself might be the father of such a slave child. If he did not need them on his own land then these slave children could simply be sold.

Because they were black, spoke strange languages and were not Christian, the white people could claim they were inferior* and that it was therefore all right to keep them as slaves. Slave-owners could not admit that blacks were equal human beings to themselves. If they did that they could not defend slavery. For the first eighty-five years of the USA, slave-owners argued that there was no disagreement or contradiction between the ideas of freedom expressed in the Declaration of Independence and the keeping of slaves. In time many farmers came to depend for their prosperity on the work of their slaves. Slavery was very profitable for everybody involved except of course for the slaves themselves.

Source D

The slave trade left a bloodstained legacy. During the four centuries the trade was pursued, it wrecked the social and economic life of Africa, set nation against nation and village against village. The trade was no less disastrous in Europe and America where it left a legacy of ill will and guilt and a potentially explosive racial problem.

(This is how one modern black American historian summed up the slave trade)

Eli Whitney's cotton gin solved the problem of how to separate the seeds from the cotton fibre as quickly as possible. New textile machinery in Britain during the Industrial Revolution increased demand for raw cotton. In the south of the USA 'cotton was king' and the basis of white people's wealth.

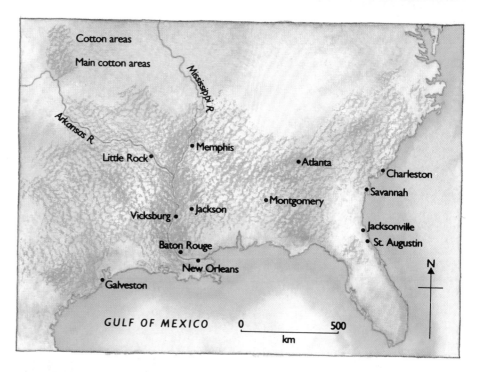

Charleston in South Carolina was one of the important ports of entry for African slaves. It became a very prosperous city, famous for its splendid buildings and graceful way of life. Just ten minutes' walk from this 1831 scene of the East Battery on the sea front was one of the largest slave markets. The import of slaves was banned in 1809 but the sale and use of slaves continued for a further fifty-seven years.

Source E

The brutal truth is this: without the slave labour of 10 million Africans, the Americas would not have been developed.

(This is the opinion of another modern historian)

What does this chapter tell us about:

● *How black people came to live in America?*
● *The way they were treated by white people?*
● *How black people felt towards whites?*

Slavery in the South

This map shows the cotton growing areas in the southern states of the USA and the cities that were the centres of cotton and slave trading.

CAUSES AND CONSEQUENCES: THE EFFECT OF THE SLAVE TRADE

1 List three reasons why slaves were used in the cotton industry.
2 Why did white people support slavery?
3 List two short and two long-term consequences of slavery.
4 What do you think was the most important consequence of slavery?

5 How do you think black Americans today might feel about the way their ancestors went to America?
6 Why do you think slavery continued in America but was banned in British colonies?

Slavery in the Caribbean

Source A

Columbus was impressed with the West Indies and wrote about 'the fair and sweet smell of flowers and trees from this land, the sweetest in the world', and the natives, he said, 'invite you to share anything that they possess and show as much love as if their hearts went with it'. Columbus thought they would make good workers.

(Extracts from the log of Christopher Columbus, 1492)

PIDGIN

A language that is a mixture of two other languages.

Columbus landing in the West Indies and meeting friendly native Caribs for the first time. Many of these native people later fought against the white people who took over their islands. Thousands of Caribs were killed.

● *Why were Africans taken to the Caribbean islands?*
● *What happened to them there?*
● *How did they react to the way they were treated?*

Thousands of Africans were taken to be slaves in the West Indies. These are a chain of islands in the Caribbean Sea. In 1492 Christopher Columbus was the first European to reach these islands. However, he thought he was actually near India so he called the islands the West Indies. He also mistakenly called the natives living there 'Indians'. Soon European nations claimed that they owned these islands in what they called the 'New World'. They argued about which country was to control the different islands. Some islands changed hands several times.

Rum and slavery

Many important crops could be grown that were much in demand in Europe. Soon natives were labouring to grow tobacco in St Kitts and sugar, often known as 'white gold', in Barbados. In 1600 the Spanish invented a new drink, rum, made from sugar, and it became very popular in Europe. There were not enough local natives and so the sugar planters began to bring in African slaves. Without these slaves they could not expand production and increase their profits. The slaves were made to work on the plantations growing the sugar-cane. Then they turned the cane into a thick syrup called molasses. In turn the molasses was made into rum to be sold in Europe.

Life for a slave was not only brutal but usually short as well. Slaves were cheap and sugar was a very profitable crop. Slaves were thought of as property and so the owners thought they could do what they liked with them. Dead slaves could be easily replaced. On the island of Antigua, it was said that slaves rarely lived for more than nine years after their arrival. What mattered to the white overseers who ran the plantations was to make the slaves work as hard as possible and to keep tight control over them. This was often done by vicious punishments. Overseers thought that with these methods more sugar would be produced even if some slaves died. Here are two pieces of evidence:

Source B

This is how the slaves were treated:
● forbidden to speak their own language and instead forced to learn some pidgin* English
● made to answer to a new non-African name chosen for them by their 'owner'
● not allowed to practise their traditional religion
● forced to work for long hours in the fields

Source C

I have heard many overseers say: 'I have made my employer 20, 30 and 40 more hogsheads [barrels] of sugar than any of my predecessors ... and though I have killed thirty or forty Negroes per year or more, yet the produce has been more than adequate to that loss.'

(A slave overseer giving evidence to the British Parliament in 1791)

Supplying the growing population in Europe with sugar and rum was very profitable. Many plantations were owned by landlords who lived in England and never visited the West Indies. They employed overseers to run them. So long as they made a good profit they did not worry about the condition of the slaves.

A map of the West Indies today

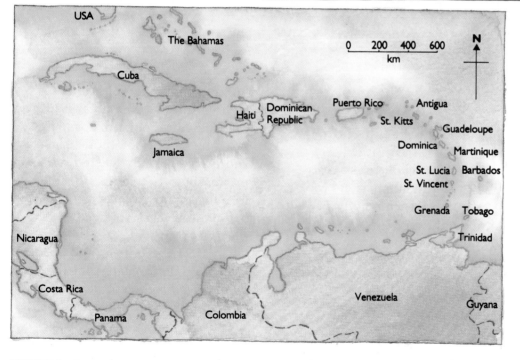

Source D

A sugar plantation. This is a Spanish sugar plantation using native slaves. You can see the different processes at work to turn sugar cane into molasses. This was then made into rum.

Source E

The number of slaves went up rapidly:

Barbados
1645   **5,680** African slaves
1667   **82,023** African slaves

Source F

Over one hundred years later, by the 1780s, this was the estimated population of the West Indies:
455,664 blacks
 65,300 whites
 20,000 mixed race

EVIDENCE: SLAVERY IN THE CARIBBEAN

1   Look at Sources E and F. How important were slaves for West Indian businesses? Explain your answer.
2   Read Sources B and C. How were slaves treated by their owners?
3   Which of Sources B and C is most useful for the study of slave conditions?
4   Do you think Source C is reliable? Explain your answer.
5   What are the advantages and disadvantages of using Source D as evidence of slave conditions?
6   What evidence on these pages would you use to support an argument against slavery?

🖺 Slave rebellions

Sometimes the African slaves in the West Indies fought back against the whites who treated them so badly. In Jamaica, after the British took it from Spain, many slaves fled into the hills to live a free life in the dense forests. These people were known as 'maroons', which comes from the Spanish word meaning 'wild'.

Source G

Good God, who makest the sun to light us from on high, who raisest up the sea and makest the storm to thunder – good God who watches over all, hidden in a cloud, protect and save us from what the white men do to us.

Good God, the white men do crimes, but we do not.

Good God, give us vengeance, guide our arms, give us help.

Negroes show the image of the good God to the white men, that we thirst not.

Good God, grant us that freedom which speaks to all men!

(This was a well-known West Indian prayer, known as 'Bon Dieu')

The slaves rebel in Haiti

The greatest revolt by slaves against their white masters took place in the French colony of Haiti. At midnight on 22 August 1791, 100,000 slaves rose up in a revolution* to seize their freedom. They attacked farmhouses, set fire to plantations and killed some of the slave-owners.

Source H

Picture to yourself the whole horizon a wall of fire, from which continually rose thick whirls of smoke ... flames which rose darting and flashing to the very sky ... for nearly three weeks we could barely distinguish between day and night, for so long as the rebels found anything to feed the flames, they never ceased to burn.

(A description by a French plantation-owner)

*
REVOLUTION
A violent uprising of people against the system that governs them.

Source I
Toussaint L'Ouverture

Pierre Dominique Toussaint L'Ouverture was the great leader of the Haitian revolution. For many years he had been a model slave and was absolutely trusted by his master. But at the age of nearly fifty he organised a superb battalion of black soldiers to win their freedom.

In 1794 the British tried to take over Haiti. Four years later they were forced to accept defeat and withdraw. Forty thousand British lives were lost as a result of disease and attacks by Toussaint's army.

In the end Toussaint became a prisoner of the French and was taken to a prison in France where he died. But by then the slaves of Haiti had gained their freedom. Their revolution frightened slave-owners everywhere. It proved that slaves could be dangerous because they were treated unjustly.

Source J

William Wilberforce (below) was a British Member of Parliament. He hated slavery and campaigned hard against it. In 1807 Parliament agreed with him and the British involvement in the slave trade was stopped.

Finally in 1833, largely thanks to Wilberforce and the Anti-Slavery Society, Parliament ended slavery altogether in the islands it controlled. Slave-owners were given twenty million pounds in compensation. In fact, because slaves outnumbered whites and because of the danger of rebellions, it was no longer safe to keep slaves.

This painting, *Kneeling Slave*, has the slogan of the British Anti-Slavery Society. During the early nineteenth century it was used in their campaign against slavery in the British Empire.

What does this chapter tell us about:
- *the reasons for slavery in the West Indies?*
- *the treatment of the slaves?*
- *the ways black people resisted slavery?*

Slaves in the British Empire were given their freedom in 1833. The plantation-owners were paid £20 million compensation! In this drawing the slaves are being told that they are now free.

Source K

Ending of slavery in the Caribbean:

British-controlled islands such as	Jamaica	**1833**
	Barbados	**1833**
	Trinidad	**1833**
French islands such as	Martinique	**1848**
	Guadeloupe	**1848**
	Puerto Rico	**1873**
	Cuba	**1888**

SLAVERY IN THE CARIBBEAN

Look back over the whole chapter and answer these questions:

1 Why was sugar known as 'white gold'?
2 Why did the number of slaves in Barbados increase so much?
3 Why do you think the slaves were not allowed to speak their own language and were given a new name?
4 Why were the runaway slaves called 'maroons'?
5 What does the prayer, Source G, tell us about the attitude of the black slaves towards the white man?
6 What effect do you think the revolution in Haiti would have had on slave-owners in other countries? Explain your answer.

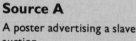

* **SUBSISTENCE**

The minimum for keeping alive.

Life as a slave

● *What was the life of black people like?*
● *What was the purpose of slavery?*
● *What was it like to work as a slave?*
● *Did slaves simply accept the way they were treated?*

The idea of human beings being owned by others as slaves will probably shock you. In chapter two we saw how large numbers of Africans were taken against their will to America. In this chapter we will study the conditions of their lives in the USA. You should use the evidence in this chapter to test the hypotheses you formed in chapter one. You should also examine whether the lives of the black slaves contradicted the ideals of the USA as set out in the Declaration of Independence.

Slavery was a cruel system in which the unwilling slaves had no rights. Some slaves fell into the hands of brutal masters from which the law gave them no protection. There was no respect for slave marriages and slave families were frequently split up. The slaves' standard of living, that is their food and homes, were usually at subsistence* level. Supporters of slavery often argued that slaves were better treated than many English farm or factory workers. But the slaves had no rights at all and they had been forcibly taken from their homeland. This is what a Bishop told slaves in a sermon in the eighteenth century:
'Your bodies, you know, are not your own; they are at the disposal of those you belong to.'

Source A

A poster advertising a slave auction

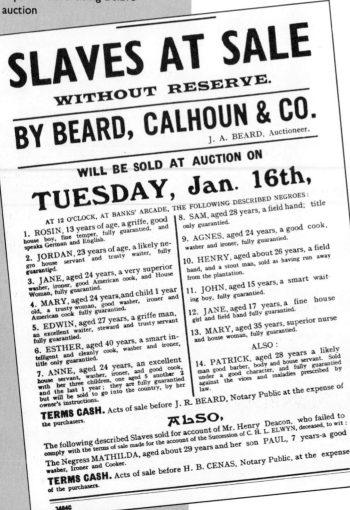

Selling female slaves by the pound

Source B

Sometimes I feel like a motherless child
Sometimes I feel like a motherless child
Sometimes I feel like a motherless child
A long ways from home
A long ways from home.

These words were part of a song the slaves sang as they worked in the fields. These sorrowful songs are called 'spirituals'* and they tell us a great deal about the feelings and suffering of the slaves.

Once they arrived in America the black slaves were sold like animals at an auction. Throughout their entire lives the slaves were bought and sold just like any other piece of property.

It is very difficult for us today to understand the horror of the slave sales. However, in 1853 a former slave, Solomon Northrup, wrote about his experiences. In his book, *Twelve Years a Slave*, he described a slave sale where children were sold separately from their parents. In the extract below, Eliza was a young mother with a small son, Randall, and a daughter, Emily. They were being sold by a slave-owner named Freeman. These are the words of Solomon Northrup who actually witnessed what happened:

Source C

The same man also purchased Randall. The little fellow was made to jump and run across the floor. Eliza pleaded with the man not to buy him unless he also bought herself and Emily. She promised, in that case, to be the most faithful slave that ever lived. The man answered that he could not afford it, and then Eliza burst into a paroxysm of grief, weeping plaintively. Freeman turned round to her, savagely, with his whip in his uplifted hand, ordering her to stop her noise, or he would flog her ... he would take her to the yard and give her a hundred lashes. She wanted to be with her children, she said, the little time she had to live.

She kept on begging and beseeching them most piteously, not to separate the three. Over and over again she told them how she loved her boy. But it was of no avail; the man could not afford it. The bargain was agreed upon, and Randall must go alone. Then Eliza ran to him; embraced him passionately; kissed him again and again; told him to remember her – all the while her tears falling in the boy's face like rain.

(Adapted from *Twelve Years a Slave* by Solomon Northrup, 1853)

Scenes like this happened many times. Another slave, Laura Clark, remembered how at the age of six she was parted from her mother in North Carolina and taken further south to be sold in Alabama. This is how she described her mother's cries:

Source D

'Take keer my baby chile (dat was me) and iffen I never sees her no mo', raise her for God.' Then her mother fell from the wagon in which the children were being carted away and 'rolled on de groun' jes' a cryin'. Laura never saw her mother again.

Source E

A slave sale

This illustration shows a mother and child for sale to different bidders. Slave children were often sold separately from their parents to serve in fashionable households.

---

* SPIRITUAL

A religious folk song that expressed the suffering and hopes of the black slaves.

BACON WANTED.

I WISH TO PURCHASE

8000 LBS. GOOD BACON, PRINCIPALLY MIDLINGS.   WM. PRITCHARTT.
                                        68——8t.
Lex. March 22d.

Negroes For Sale.

A negro woman, about 20 years of age, a boy of about 16, and one of 5 or 6 years of age, are offered for sale for cash. For further information apply at this office.
                        Lex March 23 1824.——68—tf.

Source F

Black people were bought and sold just like bacon, as this advertisement from a Kentucky newspaper in 1824 shows. It is impossible not to feel very sad when you read accounts like these.

EVIDENCE: UNDERSTANDING THE LIFE OF A SLAVE

1   What advantages and disadvantages do the written sources and illustrations have in helping us to understand the life of a slave?

2   How reliable are Sources C and D?
3   How can these sources be useful to an historian?

Life on the plantation

Throughout the southern part of North America large plantation farms were set up to grow tobacco, cotton or rice, most of it for sale to Europe. This is what a plantation was like:

Source G

The big white house stands in colonnaded splendor on a hill which overlooks fields fleeced with cotton or lined with tobacco or sugar-cane or rice. Near this house huddle two rows of log and daub cabins. Other houses and buildings dot the landscape: the overseers'* quarters, the stables, the corn cribs, the gin and press. The center of this agricultural factory is the big house. From it radiate like spokes the fields and gardens.

(This description of a nineteenth-century plantation is by a modern black historian)

Most blacks were slaves on large or small plantations. The purpose of slavery was to supply cheap labour for the plantation-owners. Life for a slave was harsh and unpleasant even if the slave-owner was not especially brutal. Black labour was thought ideal for the hot and hard conditions in the fields. After all, the climate was rather like it was in Africa. The

Source H

Homes like this one in South Carolina were built during the early nineteenth century by plantation-owners to show off their wealth and importance.

power of the masters over their slaves was almost unlimited. Usually they left it to overseers to run their estates and manage the slaves. Nearly all of them used the whip to control the slaves. Although slave-owners were not supposed to actually kill a slave, little would happen to them if they did. A court would not convict a white who had killed a black. Black people were not allowed to give evidence against whites in court.

Source I

Africans are nothing but brutes, and they will love you better for whipping, whether they deserve it or not.

(A plantation-owner in the nineteenth century describing how he treats his slaves)

Source J

Floggings of 50–75 lashes were not uncommon. On numerous occasions, planters branded, stabbed, tarred and feathered, burned, shackled, tortured, maimed, crippled, mutilated, and castrated their slaves. Thousands of slaves were flogged so severely that they were permanently scarred.

(A modern historian)

---

* **OVERSEER**

A man who directed the work of the slaves.

This nineteenth-century drawing shows a slave owner supervising the beating of a slave by other slaves. Brutal punishments were meant to ensure complete obedience.

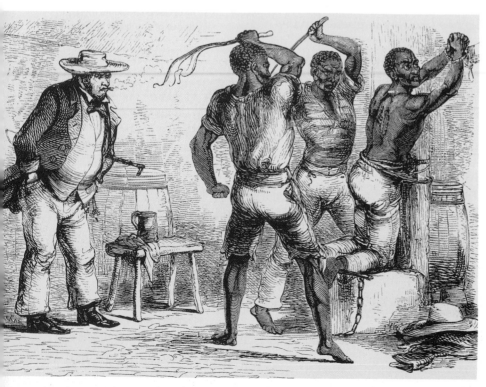

Working in the fields

Cotton was the most important crop grown in the southern states and made many farmers extremely wealthy. In 1793 the USA produced 10,000 bales of cotton; by 1800 production had risen to 100,000 bales. A great deal of this cotton was purchased by the Lancashire cotton mills in England. The slaves had to work very long hours under the hot sun to bring in the cotton crop. Children as young as six years old were forced to work in the fields. They would be woken at daybreak, sometimes as early as 4 a.m., by bells or horns. Thirty minutes later they were trudging to the cotton fields. Anyone who was late would be whipped. Then they would work all day with perhaps only one fifteen-minute break. Summer temperatures could be over a hundred degrees. Anyone who didn't seem to work hard enough would be beaten by the overseers. As well as whips, these men were also armed with guns and knives. They were usually on horseback and were often accompanied by vicious dogs.

The end of the working day came when it was too dark to continue. Then the slaves would struggle back to their living-quarters. There they would have to light a fire and prepare a meal. This was their way of life every day except Sundays. Only then could they have a little rest, and many found comfort in worshipping God. All the time they had the fear of more punishment or perhaps worse, being sold away from their families and friends.

Slave quarters

The slaves lived in small cabins about 5 metres by 5½ metres built out of bricks or wood.

Source K

This nineteenth-century etching shows slaves working in the fields

Source L

Wooden floors were an unknown luxury. In a single room were huddled, like cattle, ten or a dozen persons, men, women, and children ... There were neither bedsteads nor furniture ... Our beds were collections of straw and old rags ... The wind whistled and the rain and snow blew in through the cracks, and the damp earth soaked in the moisture till the floor was miry as a pigsty.

(This is how one slave, Joseph Henson, remembered living conditions in the 1850s)

Source M
Slave quarters

This slave house was fairly solid – which is why it is still standing today – but most were not as good as this one. Large numbers of people would live in the single room these houses contained.

* **INSURRECTION**

  An open revolt against authority.

* **OPPRESSED**

  Being unjustly treated.

Nat Turner was arrested and hanged after he led a slave revolt. White southerners were increasingly frightened that their slaves would rise up against them. This picture shows Nat Turner's capture.

Slave rebellions

You read in chapter three that there were many slave revolts in the Caribbean and some of them had been successful. At the root of these rebellions was the basic desire for freedom. There is no doubt that revolts and the increasing cost and difficulties of controlling slaves in the West Indies were important reasons for the ending of slavery in the British Empire.

In the USA the slaves had heard and celebrated the news of rebellions in the Caribbean. Resistance was dangerous but nevertheless in various ways slaves fought back against their white masters. Although there were whites who campaigned for an end to slavery it was the victims, the slaves themselves, who showed great courage and tenacity in their determination to bring about their own freedom.

By 1860 there were about four million slaves and eight million white people living in the southern United States. These population figures might help you to understand why tough Black or Slave Codes were brought in.

Source N

SLAVES
ARE NOT ALLOWED TO
* OWN PROPERTY
* LEARN TO READ AND WRITE
* BUY OR SELL GOODS
* HIT A WHITE PERSON EVEN IN SELF-DEFENCE
* ASSEMBLE IN GROUPS OF MORE THAN FIVE

(This is a summary of various laws passed in the southern states)

In spite of these strict rules and the terrible punishments for those who broke them, some slaves did rebel against their white masters. Slavery and brutal treatment had not broken the spirit of black Americans. We know that there were more than two hundred and fifty slave revolts in the USA from the sixteenth century to 1860.

Source O

Jerusalem, Virginia, November 11
Nat Turner, a slave, was hanged today for the crime of organizing and leading a revolt that resulted in the deaths of more than fifty whites.

In August, Turner incited a group of about thirty slaves from Southampton County in Virginia to kill whites. Whites in the County responded to the insurrection* by forming a force of some 3,000 armed men to pursue the Negro rebels. They killed many of the rebels, but they also killed many Negroes whose only connection with the rebels was the color of their skin. Nat Turner managed to escape and remained at large until his recent capture.

(A newspaper report of 1831)

Source P

Strike for your lives and liberties ... You cannot be more oppressed* than you have been – you cannot suffer greater cruelties than you have already. Rather die free men than live to be slaves. Remember that you are FOUR MILLIONS.

(Henry Highland Garnet, called on southern slaves to rebel in 1843)

The 'underground railway'

Many slaves tried to run away to freedom. Between 1830 and 1860 about 2,500 slaves each year travelled to freedom along an escape system to the north known as the 'underground railway'. It wasn't a railway at all. It was a secret route along which helpers led runaway slaves. They travelled ten to twenty miles by night in wagons with false bottoms. During the day they were hidden in barns, attics and haylofts. Harriet Tubman, herself a former slave, made twenty dangerous trips to help free more than two hundred slaves. Southern slave-owners put their losses at two hundred thousand dollars a year. Any slave caught trying to escape faced a terrible beating, sometimes even to death. Many white people in the North supported the 'underground railway' and large amounts of money were raised to support it.

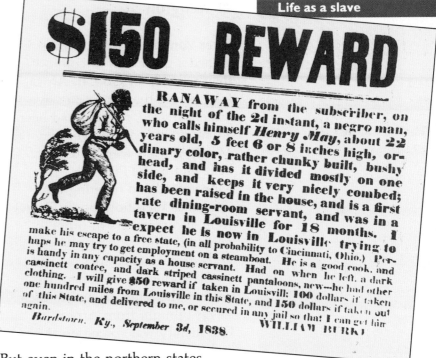

$150 REWARD

RANAWAY from the subscriber, on the night of the 2d instant, a negro man, who calls himself *Henry May*, about 22 years old, 5 feet 6 or 8 inches high, ordinary color, rather chunky built, bushy head, and has it divided mostly on one side, and keeps it very nicely combed; has been raised in the house, and is a first rate dining-room servant, and was in a tavern in Louisville for 18 months. I expect he is now in Louisville trying to make his escape to a free state, (in all probability to Cincinnati, Ohio.) Perhaps he may try to get employment on a steamboat. He is a good cook, and is handy in any capacity as a house servant. Had on when he left, a dark cassinett contee, and dark striped cassinett pantaloons, new—he had other clothing. I will give $50 reward if taken in Louisville; 100 dollars if taken one hundred miles from Louisville in this State, and 150 dollars if taken out of this State, and delivered to me, or secured in any jail so that I can get him again.

Bardstown, Ky., September 3d, 1838. WILLIAM BURK.

But even in the northern states where there was no slavery they were not safe. Fugitive* slaves, as they were known, could still be sent back south to their masters. Many had to travel on to Canada for safety.

Source Q

Advertisements like this one became common in southern newspapers. Although it was dangerous trying to escape, thousands of slaves fled to freedom.

PEOPLE IN THE PAST: THE LIFE OF A SLAVE

1 What were the worst features of the life of a slave?
2 What was the attitude of the slave-owners towards their slaves?
3 Why did many slave-owners and overseers treat their slaves so brutally?

4 Explain how the system of slavery led to violence and rebellion.
5 How did the period of slavery affect the attitudes of black and white people towards each other in America?

* FUGITIVE

Someone who is escaping.

🗐 Religion

Black Americans have always gained a great deal of comfort from their worship of God. In Africa, long before the European slave-traders arrived, religion had been an important part of everyday life. Many Africans were Muslims, believing in the Prophet Muhammad and revering the Qur'an as their holy book. There were also members of other religions, who worshipped various gods or dead ancestors.

Slave-owners tried hard to destroy the religious beliefs their slaves brought from Africa. Christianity was forced on them and they were forbidden to worship in any other ways. Sometimes slaves pretended to worship as Christians while secretly worshipping their own gods. In the West Indies some slaves adapted Christian ceremonies so they could pray to their own gods without their white masters realising. Slowly African religions began to influence Christianity in the Americas in many ways that can still be seen today.

Some slaves found it difficult to accept the religion that was practised by the slave-owners:

Source S

No sir, white men treat us so bad in Mississippi that we can't be Christians.

(Said by one runaway slave in the nineteenth century)

Even so, Christianity, with its promise of heaven after a life of suffering, did have a strong appeal. Later in the nineteenth and also during the twentieth century, black churches gave support, hope and comradeship in the face of racial discrimination. Some black Christian preachers, such as Martin Luther King, came forward to give leadership in the campaign to get equality and freedom.

A black Christian congregation in the nineteenth century

RELIGION AND SLAVERY

1 Why do you think slave-owners tried to stop the slaves following their own religions?

2 What do you think the slave in Source S meant?

3 Can you suggest reasons why many black Americans have become active Christians?

The importance of music

Music has always been a vital part of Afro-American worship. This is how one writer has described the music of black worshippers: 'it is the most original and beautiful expression of human life and longing yet born on American soil'.

Great hymns, known as 'spirituals', grew up among the slaves. They sang them in the fields as they worked, or outside their huts at night, as well as on Sundays. These songs are about the suffering of the slaves and their belief that God would help them, if not in this world then in heaven. They were really 'freedom songs'. They helped to give the slaves strength.

Source T

We'll soon be free.
We'll soon be free.
We'll soon be free.

We'll soon be free
When de Lord will call us home.
My brudder, how long,
My brudder, how long,
My brudder, how long
'Fore we done sufferin' here?
It won't be long (*thrice*)
'For de Lord will call us home.
We'll walk de miry road (*thrice*)
Where pleasure never dies.
We'll walk de golden street (*thrice*)
Where pleasure never dies.
My brudder how long (*thrice*)
'Fore we done sufferin' here?
We'll soon be free (*thrice*)
When Jesus sets me free.
We'll fight for liberty (*thrice*)
When de Lord will call us home.

(Slaves were punished if they were caught singing these words, because whites thought 'we'll soon be free' meant 'free from slavery')

Source U
All my trials
Hush little baby don't you cry,
You know your mama was born to die,
All my trials, Lord, soon be over.

Too late my brothers,
Too late, but never mind,
All my trials, Lord, soon be over.

The river of Jordan is muddy and cold,
Well it chills the body, but not the soul,
All my trials, Lord, soon be over.

I've got a little book with pages three,
And every page spells liberty,
All my trials, Lord, soon be over.

('All my trials' is probably the most famous of all the slave songs. It developed in the South of the USA and later became popular in the West Indies. It has been used by many other people to express their suffering)

Source V

These songs are the articulate message of the slave to the world, they are the music of an unhappy people ... they tell of death and suffering ... Through all the sorrow of the Sorrow Songs there breathes a hope – a faith in the ultimate justice of things ... the meaning is always clear: that sometime somewhere, men will judge men by their souls and not by their skin.

(A great American black leader, W. E. B. DuBois, summing up the importance of these songs that he called 'Sorrow Songs')

Now that you have read the words of these songs, consider whether or not they help us to understand the feelings of the black slaves.

What does this chapter tell us about
● *the difference in the way of life of black and white people?*
● *the methods used to control the slaves?*
● *the feelings of the slaves?*

Source W
I want to go home
Dere's no rain to wet you
O, yes, I want to go home
Dere's no sun to burn you
O, yes, I want to go home
O, push along, believers
O, yes, I want to go home
Dere's no hard trials
O, yes, I want to go home
Dere's no whips a-crackin'
O, yes, I want to go home
My brudder on de wayside
O, push along, my brudder
O, yes, I want to go home
Where dere's no stormy weather
O, yes, I want to go home
Dere's no tribulation*
O, yes, I want to go home

(A very old slave song)

EVIDENCE: USING SONGS

1 Are these songs primary or secondary evidence?
2 Why did DuBois call them 'Sorrow Songs'?
3 What particular words or sentences in these songs tell us about suffering?
4 What does the word 'home' refer to in the song in Source W?
5 Are these songs useful historical evidence? Explain your answer.

* **TRIBULATION**
Great suffering.

Chapter five

Slavery divides the nation

● *What effect did slavery have on white Americans?*
● *How was slavery defended and criticised?*

The South defends slavery

Now that you have read about the treatment of the slaves you may find it surprising that a slave-owner could say this:

A merrier being does not exist on the face of the globe, than the Negro slave of the United States.

Southerners could admit that slavery was a 'peculiar institution', but they were not ashamed to defend slavery. From the founding of the USA in 1776, Americans argued with one another over the whole question of slavery. There were some important differences between the northern and southern states. By the middle of the nineteenth century the North was far richer than the South. The most important industries were located in the North. There was little industry in the South and they depended on the cotton plantations and the slaves to work them. In the northern states slavery disappeared but in the South the number of slaves steadily rose. In 1820 the 'Missouri Compromise' set a dividing line between the states that could have slaves and those that could not. So the USA was split between the southern slave states and the northern free states. Many Northerners, given the nickname 'Yankees' by the Southerners, were abolitionists.* They wanted to abolish slavery once and for all everywhere in the USA. Southerners argued that they should be allowed to keep slaves even if the rest of the USA did not approve.

The two graphs below help us to understand why Southerners were so determined to hold on to their slaves whatever anyone else said.

But how could people in the South defend the system of slavery? Most Southerners, even those who did not own slaves, supported slavery. Let us eavesdrop on the arguments of the 1850s (Source B).

Source A

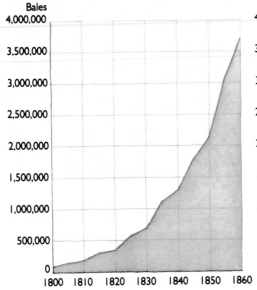

Cotton production in the southern states: 1800–1860

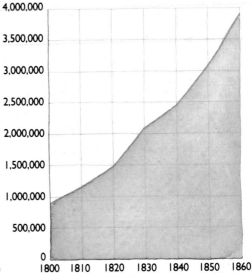

Slave population in the southern states: 1800–1860

Source B

Gentlemen, how impertinent it is for Northerners to criticise our way of life in the South. We do not tell the North how they should conduct their affairs. We do not presume to instruct them on how they should manage their factories. So why do they try to tell us how to run our plantations?

There is no doubt that many of their factory workers – white men, women and children, work in dangerous and unhealthy conditions for very low wages. Many of them are condemned to live in overcrowded and filthy housing. Yet the owners of those factories and landlords of those houses attack us for using negroes in the fields.

In the South we accept that slavery is indeed a peculiar institution. It is however vital to our prosperity and strength just as the factories are in the North.

Of course there may be some bad slave-owners just as there are bad factory owners. But I am proud that most Southern gentlemen accept their responsibilities just as you would expect any god-fearing man to do. Fate has placed the Negro in white hands for his own good. With his simple intelligence he is content to labour in the fields in return for knowing that he has all that he needs. The Negro does not have to worry about his food. The slave escapes many of the troubles that the poor have to put up with in the northern cities. The Negro never has to worry about unemployment!

Gentlemen, we are all agreed that the southern states have a complete right to run their own affairs and to make their own decisions on such matters as slavery. The government of the USA and those northern Yankees simply have no right to interfere. If they continue to try then we will have no choice but for our southern states to leave the United States.

In conclusion let me say – the rights of the South will not be trampled on!

(This made up speech summarizes the views of many Southerners in the 1850s)

Speeches like that were made all over the South. Southerners were convinced that their prosperity depended on slavery.

This nineteenth-century picture could be used to support the view expressed in Source B that the slaves were actually very happy to work in the fields for their 'kindly' white masters.

PEOPLE IN THE PAST: PRO-SLAVERY AND ABOLITIONIST

1 Why did the speaker in Source B talk about factories in the North?

2 What reasons did he put forward in support of slavery?

3 What did the speaker warn would happen if the North tried to stop slavery?

4 Do you think it was meant as a threat?

5 Do the graphs, Source A, help explain why the speaker felt so strongly in favour of slavery?

6 What do you think a 'Yankee' might have said in reply?

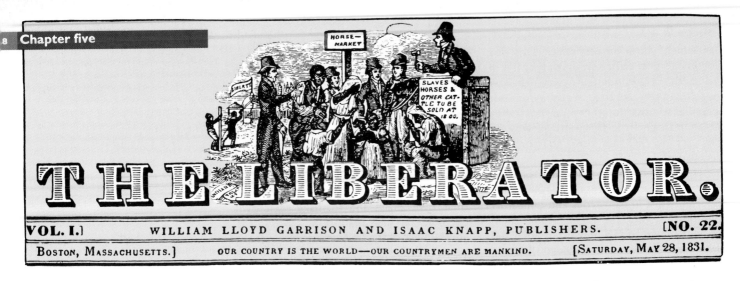

THE LIBERATOR.

VOL. I.] WILLIAM LLOYD GARRISON AND ISAAC KNAPP, PUBLISHERS. **[NO. 22.**

BOSTON, MASSACHUSETTS.] OUR COUNTRY IS THE WORLD—OUR COUNTRYMEN ARE MANKIND. [SATURDAY, MAY 28, 1831.

Source C

The Liberator was a newspaper set up by William Lloyd Garrison, a white man, in 1831 to speak out against slavery. Two years later, in Philadelphia, Garrison helped to organise the American Anti-Slavery Society. Many Northerners were abolitionists. Stories of brutality and ill-treatment of slaves reported in *The Liberator* shocked Northerners. They were angry that slavery should exist in the USA. Abolitionists used the words expressed in the Declaration of Independence (on page 5) to attack slavery.

> *** MARTYR**
>
> A person who suffers or is killed because of his or her religious or political beliefs.

≡ The abolitionists

Many different kinds of people joined together as abolitionists to stop slavery. These were some of the leading figures:

William Lloyd Garrison, from Massachusetts. He used his newspaper to fight slavery. Later he campaigned on behalf of the Native Americans and also for votes for women.

Elijah Lovejoy, a white abolitionist journalist. He was attacked many times and became a martyr when a pro-slavery mob killed him in 1837.

Source D

This is a postage stamp issued by the US Post Office to recognise the important work of Sojourner Truth.

Sojourner Truth, a runaway slave, who became a favourite speaker at abolitionist rallies. She was a deeply religious woman who spent more than forty years preaching and arguing against slavery.

Harriet Beecher Stowe, a white writer. She is most famous as the author of *Uncle Tom's Cabin,* a novel that did much to make Northerners angry over slavery.

Charles Sumner, a white US senator. He was seriously injured in the Senate when he was attacked after making a strong speech against slavery.

John Brown, a fanatical white abolitionist. In 1859 he led a raid on a government weapons store at Harper's Ferry. He planned to arm the slaves but he was captured and executed.

Frederick Douglass, a former slave. He was one of the most brilliant Americans of his time. Self-educated, he came to be the main leader of the black people in their struggle for freedom.

In spite of many differences, all these people were united by their determination to get rid of slavery. They campaigned in different ways. In those days long before radio or television the written word was very important.

Harriet Beecher Stowe's novel, *Uncle Tom's Cabin,* caused a sensation when it was published in 1852. The book condemned slavery and sold three hundred thousand copies in the first year. As you read the extract try to understand why this book was so important.

Source E

Mr Haley and Tom jogged onward in their wagon, each, for a time, absorbed in his own reflections. Now, the reflections of two men sitting side by side are a curious thing – seated on the same seat, having the same eyes, ears, hands and organs of all sorts, and having pass before their eyes the same objects – it is wonderful what a variety we shall find in these same reflections!

As, for example, Mr Haley: he thought first of Tom's length, and breadth, and height, and what he would sell for, if he was kept fat and in good case till he got him into market ... then he thought of himself and how humane he was, that whereas other men chained their 'niggers' hand and foot both, he only put fetters on the feet, and left Tom the use of his hands, as long as he behaved well; and he sighed to think how ungrateful human nature was, so that there was even room to doubt whether Tom appreciated his mercies.

(Harriet Beecher Stowe, *Uncle Tom's Cabin,* 1852)

Rallies and demonstrations were also important to stir up public interest. Listen now to Frederick Douglass, speaking at a Fourth of July (American Independence Day) celebration.

Source F

What, to the American slave, is your fourth of July? I answer; a day that reveals to him, more than all other days in the year, the gross injustice and cruelty to which he is the constant victim. To him, your celebration is a sham; your boasted liberty, an unholy license; your national greatness, swelling vanity; your sounds of rejoicing are empty and heartless; your denunciation of tyrants, brass-fronted impudence; your shouts of liberty and equality, hollow mockery; your prayers and hymns, your sermons and thanksgivings, with all your religious parades and solemnity, are to him, mere fraud, deception and hypocrisy* – a thin veil to cover up crimes which would disgrace a nation of savages.

(Extract from speech by Frederick Douglass, 4 July 1852)

● *What does this chapter tell us about the effect of slavery on America?*

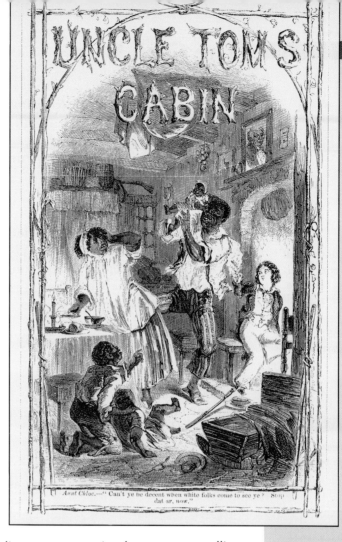

This is the frontispiece from *Uncle Tom's Cabin* (1852). It told the story of an old slave who died after being beaten by an overseer. Sometimes black people today call a black person an 'Uncle Tom' if they think he is trying too hard to please white people.

PEOPLE IN THE PAST: PRO-SLAVERY AND ABOLITIONIST

1 What were the different opinions that separated many Americans?
2 Briefly explain the main differences in the arguments between those who supported and those who opposed slavery.
3 Explain the reasons why many Southerners supported slavery and why many Northerners were against it.
4 How was America affected by the strongly held views for and against slavery?

* HYPOCRISY

Pretending to be good or to have particular beliefs when this is not so.

The Civil War

● *Was a war necessary to bring freedom to the slaves?*
● *Would black people be blamed as being the cause of the war that divided white Americans?*

Source A

A house divided against itself cannot stand ... I believe this government cannot endure, permanently half slave and half free.

(Abraham Lincoln in 1858, about the argument between the North and the South)

* CIVIL WAR

Armed conflict between groups of people who belong to the same country.

On 12 April 1861 Southern soldiers opened fire on the US Army fortress, Fort Sumter, at Charleston, South Carolina. The Civil War* between North and South that so many had feared had begun. It turned out to be a terrible war. By the time it was over, 620,000 American soldiers had died: 360,000 Union (Northern Army) and 260,000 Confederate (Southern Army). This is almost as many soldiers as have been killed in all the other wars that the United States has been involved in, such as the First and Second World Wars and the Vietnam War, added together. It was the bloodiest war anywhere in the world during the nineteenth century. Nearly every family lost a friend or relative. The South suffered worse with nearly a quarter of its white men killed and many others wounded and maimed.

The issue of slavery was not the sole cause of the American Civil War. Certainly the question of slavery was important, but the war was actually fought to stop the USA breaking into two different countries and to keep it as a single, united nation.

In November 1860 Lincoln, a member of the Republican Party, was elected President of the USA. The South was furious. Lincoln's election would, they believed, lead to the destruction of their southern way of life including slavery.

Following Lincoln's election, on 20 December 1860 the state of South Carolina took the decision to leave the United States. It was followed by ten other states. In this way a new country, known as the Confederate States of America (CSA), or the Confederacy, was created. The map opposite shows how America was divided. On 8 February 1861, the Confederacy chose their own president, Jefferson Davis. The United States were no longer united. Lincoln, as President, could not allow this break-up of the USA. So although it was slavery that had divided the North and the South, it was the southern states leaving, or seceding as it was called, that actually led to the Civil War.

Southern soldiers attack Fort Sumter, South Carolina, and the Civil War begins

CAUSES AND CONSEQUENCES: WHY WAS THERE A CIVIL WAR?

1 What did Lincoln mean in Source A by 'a house divided against itself'?
2 Why was the South angry when Lincoln was elected President?
3 Explain the causes of the war.
4 What was the most significant cause?
5 Could the Civil War have been avoided?

Now let us examine some of the different points of view about the war.

Source B
The Southern view

We fight for our homes, our fathers and mothers, our wives, brothers, sisters, sons, and daughters! We can call out a million of peoples if need be, and when they are cut down we can call another, and still another, until the last man of the South finds a bloody grave.

(Alexander Stephens, Vice President of the Confederate States of America, 1863)

Source C
A black American view

The iron gate of our prison stands half open. One gallant rush from the North will fling it wide open, while four millions of our brothers and sisters shall march out into liberty ... This is our golden opportunity. Let us accept it ... Let us win for ourselves the gratitude of our country, and the best blessings of our posterity through all time.

(Frederick Douglass, a leading black campaigner, urging blacks to join the Union Army, in a newspaper article on 2 March 1863)

Source D
President Lincoln's view

Fourscore and seven years ago our fathers bought forth on this continent a new nation, conceived in liberty, and dedicated to the proposition that all men are created equal. Now we are engaged in a great civil war, testing whether that nation ... can long endure. We are met on a great battlefield of that war ... a final resting-place for those who gave their lives that that nation might live ... we here highly resolve that these dead shall not have died in vain; that this nation, under God, shall have a new birth of freedom; and that government of the people, by the people, for the people, shall not perish from the earth.

(Part of Abraham Lincoln's speech, known as the Gettysburg Address, in 1863)

Source E
A soldier's view

War is horrid beyond the conception of man. It is enough to break the heart to go through the hospitals. Old grey-haired veterans with lips whitening under the kiss of death – hundreds of mere boys with thoughts of home ... nothing but pain, misery, neglect, and death around you, everywhere nothing but death.

(Colonel Robert Ingersoll, 1862)

This poster called for volunteers to join the Northern Army. It mentions 1776 – the year America declared its independence from Britain.

Map of the Confederacy
showing dates of secession

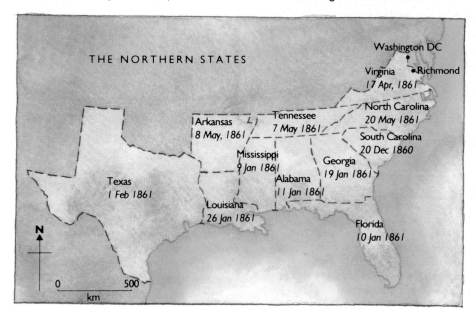

PEOPLE IN THE PAST: THE CIVIL WAR

1 How would you describe Alexander Stephens' view of the war?
2 Why did Frederick Douglass see the war as a 'golden opportunity'?
3 Explain in your own words the view of the soldier in Source E.
4 What reasons did Lincoln give in support of the war?
5 Explain why these people held differing views about the war.

The 54th Massachusetts Infantry Regiment in hand-to-hand combat on Battery Wagner, a key fortification protecting Charleston Harbour. The regiment was made up of 1,000 black soldiers but commanded by a white man, Col. Robert Gould Shaw.

More than forty per cent of the regiment was killed in this battle, including Colonel Shaw. Southern soldiers stripped his body and threw it in a ditch with his dead black troops. They intended it as an insult. Colonel Shaw's father told a newspaper: 'We can imagine no holier place than that in which he is ... nor wish him better company – what a bodyguard he has!'

Many black Americans were actually pleased when the Civil War started. This is what Frederick Douglass said:

Source F

Once let the black man get upon his person the brass letters, US, let him get an eagle on his button, and a musket on his shoulder and bullets in his pocket, and there is no power on earth which can deny that he has earned the right to citizenship in the United States.

(Frederick Douglass, 1863)

Source G

So rally, boys rally, let us never mind the past;
We had a hard road to travel, but our days is coming fast;
For God is for the right, and we have no need to fear,
The Union must be saved by the colored volunteer.

(This was a favourite camp song of black soldiers)

But it was not until 1863 that the US Government began officially to recruit black soldiers. Mixed units were unthinkable and blacks were made to serve in separate regiments. (Racial segregation in the armed forces didn't finally end until 1948.) At first black soldiers were paid only seven dollars a month instead of the thirteen dollars a white private received. Whites, even many of those who disliked slavery, looked down on blacks as inferior, and the black soldiers were not always respected. Whites still could not accept them as equal Americans with themselves. Some, like Lincoln himself for a time, thought it would be a good idea to free the slaves and then send them all to live in Central America.

Source H

I cannot bring myself to trust Negroes with arms in positions of danger and trust.

(William Sherman, an important Union general)

Some Northern soldiers blamed blacks for being the root cause of the war.

Source I

If the Negro was thought of at all in 1861, it was only as the firebrand that had caused the conflagration, the accursed that had created enmity and bitterness between the two sections and excited the fratricidal [between brothers] strife.

(This was the view of one white soldier in the Union Army expressed after the war had ended)

THE MASSACRE AT FORT PILLOW

Official Confirmation of the Report.

Three Hundred Black Soldiers Murdered After Surrender.

Fifty-three White Soldiers Killed and One Hundred Wounded.

RETALIATION TO BE MADE

This newspaper cutting tells of a famous massacre

Perhaps not surprisingly, the South took a tough view of black Union soldiers. On 23 December 1862, Confederate President Jefferson Davis proclaimed that any black captured during fighting would immediately be returned to slavery. Any black officer in US Army uniform was to be executed. At Fort Pillow, Confederate soldiers murdered three hundred black soldiers and civilians who had surrendered to them.

The Civil War was one of the very first wars to be photographed. Photographers recorded the miseries of the war as well as portraits of the soldiers. This one shows Andrew Scott, a black soldier in the Union army.

For many Americans, including blacks, it was incredible that at last black people should be wearing the uniform of their country. By their service in the US Army they were able to play an important part in freeing their own people.

Statistics

- Official records show that a total of 186,107 men served in black regiments, which was about 10% of the Union Army.
- Black soldiers fought in 449 battles.
- An additional 200,000 blacks served the Union Army as labourers, cooks and nurses.

- 37,300 blacks lost their lives while serving in the Union Army.
- 17 black Union soldiers and 4 black sailors were awarded the Congressional Medal of Honor – America's highest military award.

EVIDENCE: THE ROLE OF BLACK SOLDIERS

1 What evidence is there that many black Americans welcomed the Civil War?

2 What evidence is there that even in the army they were not treated fairly?

3 What evidence is there in this section to support the view that black Americans played a full part in the overthrow of slavery?

4 How useful is Source G?

5 How reliable and useful are Sources F, H and I in helping an historian to understand attitudes about black soldiers?

Lincoln presents the first draft of the Emancipation Proclamation to his Cabinet, 22 July 1862

🔊 Victory and freedom

The Emancipation Proclamation

On the 1st of January 1863, President Lincoln issued the Emancipation Proclamation. ('Emancipation' means the granting of freedom.) Lincoln granted freedom to the slaves and so brought to an end two hundred and fifty years of legal slavery in the USA. All slaves in the southern slave-holding states were declared free. Of course until the war was over and the South defeated it was not possible to actually free most of the slaves. But Lincoln's action made it clear that the Civil War had become a war to end slavery. Gradually word spread and we can imagine the feelings of the slaves as they heard of Lincoln's action. President Lincoln wrote out the Proclamation in his own handwriting and these are the words that he used:

Source J

That on the first day of January, in the year of our Lord 1863, all persons held as slaves within any State, or designated part of a State, the people whereof shall then be in rebellion against the United States, shall be then, thenceforward, and forever free.

(Emancipation Proclamation, 1863)

Finally in December 1865, after the surrender of the South, the 13th Amendment to the United States Constitution* became law, containing this clear statement:

Source K

Neither slavery nor involuntary servitude shall exist within the United States.

(The 13th Amendment to the US Constitution, 1865)

Tragically, just six days after the war had ended, Lincoln was shot dead by a Southern sympathiser as he watched a play at Ford's Theatre in Washington D.C.

Source L

I never seed Mr Lincoln but when they tole me 'bout him, I thought he was partly God.

(Angie Garrett, an Alabama slave)

* **CONSTITUTION**

The set of laws and rules by which a country is governed.

At the end of the war, President Lincoln visited the former Southern capital, Richmond. The freed slaves rushed to greet him. Ten days later Lincoln was assassinated in Washington D.C.

* **ASSASSINATION**

The killing of an important person.

LINCOLN AND EMANCIPATION

1 How did Lincoln make it clear that the war was about slavery?
2 Do you think it is important to know that he wrote out the Emancipation Proclamation in his own handwriting?
3 Why did Angie Garrett think Lincoln was 'partly God'?

Free at last

Throughout the South, black people who had been held in slavery all their lives could celebrate their new freedom. These are some of their descriptions of what happened when they heard they were free:

Source M

The soldiers marched in to tell us that we were free ... I remember one woman. She jumped on a barrel and she shouted some more. She kept that up for a long time, just jumping on a barrel and back off again.

(Anna Woods, a young slave in Texas)

Source N

I remember hearing my pa say that when somebody came and hollered, 'You niggers is free at last,' he just dropped his hoe and said in a queer voice, 'Thank God for that.'

(Anna Mae Weathers, a young slave)

Source O

Niggers shoutin' and clappin' hands and singin'! Chillun runnin' all over the place beatin' time and yellin'! Everybody happy. Sho' did some celebratin'. Run to the kitchen and shout in the window: 'Mammy, don't you work no more. You's free! You's free!'

(Fannie Berry, a teenage slave)

These were the feelings of black people more than two hundred years after the first Africans had been forcibly taken to America for

This famous photograph shows Abraham Lincoln with his son, Tad. Lincoln was President of the USA during the most difficult period in its history. Today Lincoln is one of the most respected figures in American history.

a life of slavery. But it had taken a terrible civil war to give these Americans their freedom.

HERE BROTHERS FOUGHT FOR THEIR PRINCIPLES

HERE HEROES DIED TO SAVE THEIR COUNTRY

AND A UNITED PEOPLE WILL FOREVER CHERISH

THE PRECIOUS LEGACY OF THEIR NOBLE MANHOOD

Source P

These words are on a monument at the Vicksburg Battlefield. Six hundred and twenty thousand Americans – many of them young men – had died in the Civil War. The big question that faced America was whether they could really be a united people. Would bitterness between the North and South remain?

PEOPLE IN THE PAST: THE END OF SLAVERY

1   How do you think Northerners and Southerners felt at the end of the Civil War about the defeat of the South and the ending of slavery?
2   Which people would not have been happy that the slaves had been freed?
3   Do you think that relations between black and white people in the South

were likely to be good after the war? Explain your reasons.
4   Put yourself in the position of either a Union or a Confederate soldier at the end of the war. Write a letter to your family telling them how you feel about the victory or defeat of your side in the war.

SUMMARY: THE AMERICAN CIVIL WAR 1861–65

Arrange these events in the correct chronological order:
a   Assassination of President Lincoln.
b   Emancipation of the slaves.
c   Attack on Fort Sumter.
d   The 13th Amendment to the US Constitution.
e   Setting up the Confederate States of America.
f   Election of President Lincoln.
g   Surrender of the South.

* **LEGACY**

Something handed down from the past.

From slavery to freedom

Source A

The destruction and fall of the southern capital of Richmond, 1865. A photo of the ruins of Richmond can be seen below.

Source B

Oh, I'm a good old rebel,
Now that's just what I am,
For the fair land of freedom
I do not care a damn.
I'm glad I fit against it –
I only wish we'd won
And I don't want no pardon
For anything I done.

(A song from the South at the end of the war)

● *Could Americans forgive each other after the war?*
● *Did the end of slavery mean equality for black people with white Americans?*

The slaves were free but how were they going to live? How were they going to be treated by their former white masters? Would white people, especially in the South, accept blacks as equal citizens? Would black and white people live peaceably alongside one another? These questions faced Americans at the end of the Civil War. The answers have worried and divided Americans ever since.

The war had left a great deal of bitterness in the defeated South. Southerners directed their resentment against the newly freed slaves.

Reconstruction

Reconstruction is the name given to the period of American history after the Civil War. It is also known as the 'Tragic Era'.

Much of the South had to be rebuilt. Railroad lines had been torn up; towns and cities burnt down; plantations destroyed by the fighting. Northern politicians and government officials were sent into the South to organise elections and set up new state governments. Southerners disliked these men because they represented the victorious North. They called them 'carpetbaggers' – meant as an insult – because many of them arrived carrying bags made from carpet material. Black men were now allowed to vote and take part in the government of their country. This too was disliked by white Southerners.

Soon black politicians were elected to state and local governments. But most blacks were poor, uneducated and had no political experience either as voters or as politicians. Unfortunately, there was a great deal of corruption. A few mostly Northern businessmen made large profits out of overcharging on contracts to repair war damage. The people who benefited were nearly always white, but black politicians and carpetbaggers took the blame. Perhaps it should be remembered that corruption was quite common in American politics in the North as well as in the South. White Southerners were quick to criticise black politicians because they wanted them to fail.

Different views of Reconstruction

Often historians cannot agree about particular events. There are different views about the period of Reconstruction. Here are two historians who criticise Reconstruction:

Source C

The Negro-carpetbagger governments were the most wasteful and inefficient ever known in an English-speaking land.

(A modern white American historian)

Source D

There now came into being state governments marked by a degree of corruption such as the world has rarely seen, legislatures often controlled by black majorities whose members regarded it as their essential business to fill their pockets.

(A modern white British historian)

But is this entirely fair? There is a different view. This one is by a modern black historian:

Source E

Reconstruction had an immediate impact on the lives of black Americans ... a significant number of blacks climbed a rung or two on the economic ladder ... they created a public system in a region hostile to public education ... the monstrous crime of Reconstruction was equality ... Southern whites feared good black government.

Finally, here is another historian's view that sees positive benefits from Reconstruction:

Source F

The Reconstruction governments in the southern states left memories, set precedents [examples], and inspired hope for the future. All too briefly, black citizens had voted, had held office, and had participated actively in political life ... but the odds had been heavily stacked against them.

(A modern white British historian)

As you can see, Reconstruction remains a controversial* part of American history. That it failed is clear. Reconstruction stands out as a period of lost opportunity. Southern whites were determined that in spite of their defeat, white supremacy would be restored. Northerners did not want the question of black rights to stand in the way of white Americans, North and South, working together to create a prosperous USA. For their part, the former slaves could see that the full meaning of their freedom had not been achieved.

* CONTROVERSIAL

Something which there is argument and disagreement over.

The first black politicians

FROM THE PLANTATION TO THE SENATE.

DIFFERENT VIEWS: RECONSTRUCTION

1 What criticisms were made of Reconstruction governments?
2 Do you think the writer of Source E really thought equality was a 'monstrous crime'?
3 Do Sources D, E, and F tell us facts or opinions?

4 Explain the differences between the views expressed in Sources C and D and those in E and F.
5 Why do you think historians may have difficulty agreeing about what happened during Reconstruction?

ᨆᨆ **Sharecroppers**

The blacks who had been slaves now had to earn their living. Many of them did not want to work for wages because it kept them under the direction of whites and reminded them of slavery.

Quite quickly a new agricultural system known as sharecropping emerged. Plantation-owners broke up their estates into small parcels of land for sharecropping. In return for seed and equipment, the sharecropper would give the landlord a third or a half of his crop. Life as a sharecropper was very hard and many blacks as well as some whites were trapped by poverty. They could never raise enough cash to buy their own land and equipment. Often they would get into debt with local banks and shopkeepers.

A nineteenth-century photograph showing sharecroppers picking cotton

SHARECROPPERS

1 How had the plantation shown in Source G changed between 1860 and 1881?
2 Why had it changed?
3 Why were most sharecroppers poor?

Source G

A Georgia plantation in 1860 and in 1881

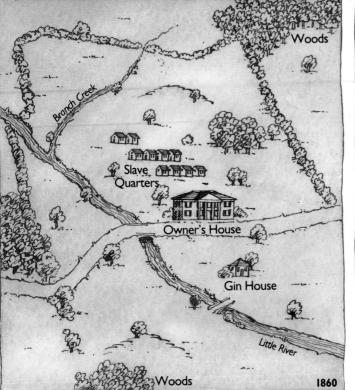

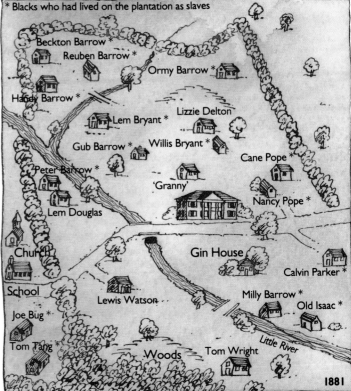

⅏ The Ku Klux Klan

Source H

Pulaski, Tennessee, December 1865
Six former Confederate soldiers have set up a new secret society. Calling itself the Ku Klux Klan – from the Greek word 'kuklos' meaning circle – they ride at night in hooded white robes. It is claimed the KKK are harmless ...

Washington DC, June 1868
A congressional Committee on Violence says that it is believed that the Ku Klux Klan has killed thousands of black people.

(Excerpts from newspapers of the time)

The Ku Klux Klan was a white underground terrorist group. They would not accept black people as equal citizens. They also wanted revenge for the defeat of the South. The KKK created a wave of terror among blacks and those whites who tried to help them. Many important politicians, officials and even police officers supported the Klan. Sometimes blacks were stopped from voting by being beaten up. Black sharecroppers had their crops stolen or destroyed.

The main aim of the Klan was to ensure white supremacy. It was very successful. The Klan's campaign of terror, including threats of violence and murder, terrified many black people so that they did not register to vote. Black and white politicians were afraid to stand up for the rights of black citizens. The power and determination of Southern whites destroyed the hopes of black people and brought the period of Reconstruction to an end. Many blacks in the South were hardly better off than when they had been slaves. Once again black Americans had to realise that they would have to struggle against racial discrimination in order to gain fair and equal treatment.

● *What does this chapter tell us about race relations after the war?*

Source I

This grim warning was drawn by the Alabama Ku Klux Klan and printed in a newspaper in 1868.

Source J

This photograph shows a modern Ku Klux Klan rally. Dressed in white robes the Klansmen are marching carrying Southern flags from the Civil War era.

PEOPLE IN THE PAST: THE 'TRAGIC ERA'

1 How does Source I help us to understand the feelings of southern whites?
2 Why were the 'carpetbaggers' so unpopular in the South?
3 What benefits did black people gain from 'Reconstruction'?
4 Why do you think the Ku Klux Klan was formed?

5 Why do Klansmen dress up in white robes?
6 Using the information and sources explain why you think this period is sometimes called the 'Tragic Era'.
7 Put yourself in the position of a black living in the South during Reconstruction. Describe your hopes and fears.

Segregation

≋ 'Jim Crow' laws

● *How did white Southerners stop black people from having their rights as full citizens?*
● *How did black people struggle to gain their rights?*

'Jim Crow' was a character in an old song made popular by a white comedian, 'Daddy' Rice. It was also the name of a dance. In his act, Rice made fun of black people and the way they spoke, their dialect. Soon the term 'Jim Crow' came to be another insulting name given to black people. But 'Jim Crow' laws, as they became known, were something far more serious. These laws, passed in each state throughout the South, discriminated against blacks and established segregation. Segregation meant that black people were kept separate from whites. The practice of segregation made sure that black Americans continued to be treated as second-class citizens.

An important decision by the United States Supreme Court in 1896 declared that 'Jim Crow' laws were legal. Homer Plessey, a black man, challenged a Louisiana railroad company because they made him sit in a 'colored only' carriage. The Supreme Court supported the railroad company. The Court said that it was legal for facilities used by blacks and whites to be kept separate. The words the Court used were: 'separate but equal'. It was a disastrous decision for black Americans.

Encouraged by this judgement, the white South pressed ahead rapidly with 'Jim Crow' laws to cover every aspect of life. Soon signs like the ones below became normal.

For fifty-eight years segregation in many parts of America was normal *and* legal. Black citizens were stopped from using the same facilities as whites in restaurants, hotels, theatres and cinemas. Many states also forbade marriage between black and white people. Separate, and always inferior, schools were set up for black children. Separate black and white residential areas in towns were created. There was even segregation in the armed forces, and the American Red Cross kept black people's blood segregated in blood banks until the 1940s. Ways were even found to prevent most black people from having the right to vote.

Source A
Jim Crow
Weel a-bout and turn a-bout
And do just so.
Every time I weel a-bout
I jump Jim Crow.

(A nineteenth-century song)

Source B
Southern notices demonstrating segregation

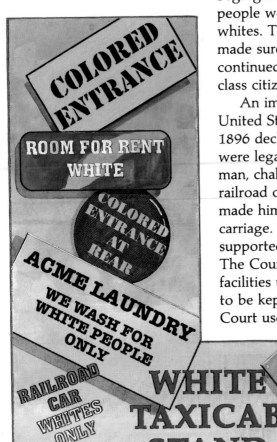

Source C
Two ways black Americans were stopped from voting:
● **Poll tax:** A tax on every person that many poor blacks could not afford to pay. Failure to pay meant they were not allowed to vote.

● **Literacy tests:** People had to explain the meaning of a legal document in order to qualify to vote. Blacks who dared to take the test were nearly always said to have failed it.

This is what happened in Louisiana:
1896 election   **130,000** blacks voted
1900 election   **5,000** blacks voted*

(* after the Supreme Court ruling)

Source D
We take away the Negroes' votes to protect them just as we would protect a little child and prevent it from injuring itself with sharp-edged tools.

(A Louisiana politician in 1900)

So long as whites in the South could have segregation they could forget some of their bitterness over their defeat in the Civil War. White people of the North and South could be friends again, but at the expense of black people.

PEOPLE IN THE PAST: SEGREGATION

1   What does the word 'segregation' mean?
2   Why were segregation laws known as 'Jim Crow' laws?
3   Why do you think white people in the South were so keen to have segregation?
4   How did whites take away the right of black people to vote?
5   Do you think these methods were unfair? Explain your answer.
6   How do you think black people felt as segregation laws were introduced?

≈ 'Keep the Negro in his place'

The most horrible results of this campaign to 'keep the Negro in his place' were the lynchings that took place. Black people accused of crimes were often taken out and hanged or even burned to death before they could be brought to trial. On many occasions the police made little or no effort to stop it happening. Many of the victims were probably innocent of any crime but may have been thought of as black troublemakers. The mobs that took the law into their own hands were particularly brutal if the black was accused of assaulting a white woman. But the real purpose of the lynchings was probably to remind blacks forcibly that the whites were firmly in control.

Source E
The lynching of two black men in the South in the twentieth century

The lynching
Day dawned, and soon the mixed crowds
   came to view
The ghastly body swaying in the sun:
The women thronged to look, but never a one
Showed sorrow in her eyes of steely blue;
And little lads, lynchers that were to be,
Danced round the dreadful thing in
   fiendish glee.

(Claude McKay [1890–1948])

Source F
These figures are of the number of lynchings in some sample years between 1882–1921:

date	No. of lynchings
1882	42
1887	70
1892	161
1897	123
1903	84
1910	67
1915	56
1921	51

(Tuskegee Institute)

1952 was the first year when no lynching was reported.

EVIDENCE: LYNCHINGS

1   How useful is Source F?
2   How does Source F help us to understand what it must have been like to have been a black American living in the South?
3   How useful are photographs such as Source E to historians?
4   What are the strengths and weaknesses of the different types of sources?
5   What other sources might an historian use to find out more information about the lynchings that took place?

≋ **Two leaders: two ways forward**

In the late nineteenth and early twentieth centuries two great leaders emerged. They had quite different ideas as to how black Americans should try to improve their position. There was a lot of disagreement among black people as to whose ideas were best. As you read this think about the dilemma that faced black people.

Booker T. Washington

Booker T. Washington

Booker T. Washington was born into slavery in 1856. After gaining an education he set up the Tuskegee Institute in Alabama. His purpose was to give black people education and training so that they would be successful workers and businesspeople. Washington believed that education and economic progress were the best ways forward and *not* demands for equality. Most blacks in the South lived in poverty, but if they learnt skills, worked hard, and bought property, Washington believed that gradually they would gain civil and political rights.

As more and more blacks suffered from 'Jim Crow' laws and even lynchings, Washington told them to avoid conflict with white people. He said they should stop demanding equal rights and simply try to get along with whites. Washington said what white Americans wanted to hear (see Source G).

These views became known as the 'Atlanta Compromise'. Black people were to put up with 'Jim Crow' laws and segregation so long as they could earn fair wages and perhaps even have their own businesses. Many white people had great admiration for Washington. He was given honours, money for his work and even visited the President at the White House.

A class at the Tuskegee Institute

Source G

The wisest among my race understand that the agitation of questions is the extremist folly ... The opportunity to earn a dollar in a factory is of more importance than the opportunity to spend a dollar in the opera house.

(Booker T. Washington, Speech in Atlanta, 18 September 1895)

PEOPLE IN THE PAST: THE VIEWS AND MOTIVES OF WASHINGTON AND DuBOIS

1 Why did Booker T. Washington think black Americans should have training and education?
2 Why did Washington say blacks should avoid conflict with whites?
3 What do you think Washington meant in Source G?
4 Why do you think many white people supported Washington?
5 Describe the views known as the 'Atlanta Compromise'.
6 What did DuBois say black people should do?

7 What did DuBois mean in Source H?
8 Why do you think white people disagreed with DuBois?
9 How do the views of Washington and DuBois differ?
10 Write a short letter explaining why you support the ideas of either
   a Washington, or
   b DuBois.
11 Explain the meaning and importance of each of the principles set out in Source I.

Strong disagreement

Washington	DuBois
↓	↓
Education	Organisation
↓	↓
Hard work	Campaigns
↓	↓
Thrift	Protests
↓	↓
Good Behaviour	Refusal to give in to whites
↓	↓
Gradual acceptance by whites as equals	Put pressure on whites to give back equal rights

W.E.B. DuBois 29

Black Heritage USA

W. E. B. DuBois

W. E. B. DuBois was the great great grandson of an African slave. He strongly disagreed with Washington's approach. He too was educated. He had a degree from one of America's top universities, Harvard. DuBois was not prepared to put up with racial discrimination. He criticised Booker T. Washington for seeming to give in and not stand up for black people's rights. DuBois said the main problem at the beginning of the twentieth century was the 'problem of the color line'. He said black people must demand every right promised to Americans in the Declaration of Independence and in the US Constitution. Black people, he said, had to band together, to organise and to fight back against white racism. He wanted immediate action rather than just promises for the future.

In 1905 DuBois and about thirty other blacks met at Niagara Falls. They became known as the Niagara Movement. DuBois told them this:

Source H

In the past year the work of the Negro hater has flourished in the land. Step by step the defenders of the rights of American citizens have retreated ... We will not be satisfied to take one jot or tittle less than our full manhood rights. We claim for ourselves every single right that belongs to a freeborn American ... and until we get these rights we will never cease to protest.

(W. E. B. DuBois, Manifesto of the Niagara Movement, August 1906)

In 1910 the members of the Niagara Movement became part of a new organisation, the National Association for the Advancement of Colored People, usually known as the NAACP. Ever since, it has been a very important organisation, standing up for the rights of black people. There have been many times when the ideas of DuBois and the NAACP have not been popular with white people. Below are the eight principles of the Niagara Movement that were taken up by the NAACP.

Source I
Principles of the Niagara Movement
1   Freedom of speech and criticism.
2   An unfettered* and unsubsidized* press.
3   Male suffrage.*
4   The abolition of all caste* distinctions based simply on race and color.
5   The recognition of the principle of human brotherhood.
6   The recognition of the highest and best human training as the monopoly of no class or race.
7   A belief in the dignity of labor.
8   United effort to realize these ideals under wise and courageous leadership.

UNFETTERED

Free from any control.

UNSUBSIDIZED

Not receiving money from anyone.

SUFFRAGE

The right to vote.

CASTE

A class or group of people separated from others by some difference such as race or colour.

*

MIGRATION

The movement of people to another part of the country.

*

GHETTO

Part of a city where one particular group of people live.

≋ Migration* north

To many blacks it was becoming apparent that the South was not a good place to live. They began to look to the northern states for a better life. New industries were growing rapidly in the northern cities and taking on more workers. In the North they could enjoy a better standard of living and, so they hoped, no longer suffer from racial discrimination.

Why blacks wanted to leave the South

- Sharecropping trapped black farmers in debt and poverty.
- There were few jobs for blacks other than on the land.
- Segregation and racism stopped blacks from improving their conditions.
- The Ku Klux Klan and other whites threatened violence against black people.

1890–1910: The first migration

The first black people to move north were mainly the educated, often self-educated. They were nicknamed the 'talented tenth' of the black population. Many of them set up businesses or became lawyers in northern cities.

1910–1920: Mass migration north

In this period large numbers of ordinary black workers began to leave the land and move to the industrial northern cities. The First World War gave a great boost to many industries, and factories were desperate for extra workers. Once a black person from the South had got a job in the North this would encourage members of his family to move, and soon brothers, sisters and cousins were joining the flood northwards.

Between 1910 and 1920 about 300,000 people moved north. Even more followed them during the next ten years.

However, although there were no 'Jim Crow' laws in the North, there was still racism. White people looked down on black people, and many did not like this movement of blacks from the South. Black people were usually the last to be given a job and the first to be fired. Often the poorest-paid work was done by black workers. Even so, the opportunities for black people were much greater than in the South and the numbers moving to northern cities continued to grow.

Source J
Population of major cities

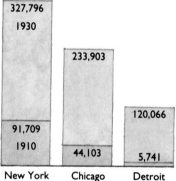

(Of course not all of this increase was simply due to black people moving to the North)

Black neighbourhoods (ghettos)* began to emerge in northern cities. Some black people headed west, and cities in California such as Los Angeles and San Francisco also began to have large black communities.

Do you think this movement from the South helped black Americans to be treated as equal citizens or was it avoiding the problem?

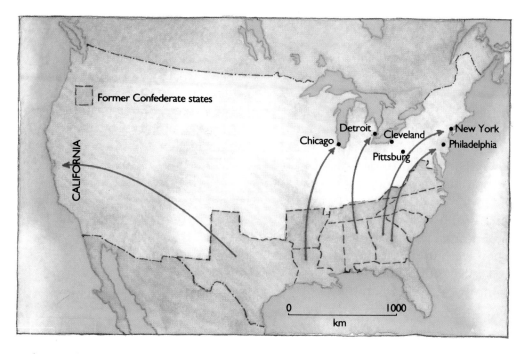

The great migration by black people to the north and west

Below is how one historian explains the real importance of the 'Great Migration':

Source K

The Great Migration was a revolt ... An idea – the idea of freedom – moved the people, sending them in ever-increasing numbers to Chicago, New York, Detroit ... In the big cities of the North blacks emancipated [freed] themselves, casting off the garments of slavery and the feudal South.

(A modern black American historian)

Source L

In one district in New York a Negro population equal in numbers to the inhabitants of Dallas, Texas, or Springfield, Massachusetts, lives, works, and pursues its ideals almost as a separate entity from the great surrounding metropolis.* Here Negro merchants ply their trade; Negro professional men follow their various vocations; their children are educated; the poor, sick, and orphan of the race are cared for; churches, newspapers, and banks flourish heedless of those, outside this Negro community, who resent its presence in a white city.

(A black writer describing Harlem around 1920)

What did this chapter tell us about:
● *how segregation made black people second-class citizens?*
● *the violence used to terrorise black people?*
● *the ways black people resisted racism?*

Black children playing in Harlem in 1930

MIGRATION TO THE NORTH

1 Why did many black people want to leave the South

2 Do you think some black people might have been disappointed in the North?

3 What is meant in source K by the 'idea of freedom'?

4 How do you think life was different in the black district described in Source L from that in the South?

5 What does the migration north tell us about the struggle of black people for proper and equal treatment?

* **METROPOLIS**

A city.

'We shall overcome'

Back to Africa

In the twentieth century, some black Americans welcomed an idea that they should 'return' to Africa. Many had begun to despair of ever getting justice or enjoying a full life in the United States. During the First World War thousands of black Americans fought for their country. They were told that the war was to make the 'world safe for democracy'.* But when they got home they found that in the South they were still prevented from voting and that segregation remained firmly in place.

Those who had moved to the North found that even there they were usually treated as second-class citizens. They could find no escape from living in slum housing or doing low-paid jobs.

Many of these people became eager followers of Marcus Garvey. Garvey, originally from Jamaica in the West Indies, believed that black people belonged in Africa, the home of their ancestors. Many black people had a strong emotional link to Africa and Garvey gained a huge following for his Universal Negro Improvement Association. He did not think there was any hope for black people in white America. He declared himself the 'Leader of the Negro Peoples of the World'. Certainly he was a very popular leader and he encouraged many black people to take pride in their race and to stand up and demand their rights.

But Garvey's dream of a 'return' to Africa by millions of black Americans never happened. He was found guilty of misusing money given to his organisation. He claimed he was innocent, but after serving two years in prison he was sent back to Jamaica.

Source A

> A message to black US soldiers:
>
> DO YOU ENJOY THE SAME RIGHTS AS THE WHITE PEOPLE DO IN AMERICA?

During the First World War the Germans dropped leaflets with this message to black soldiers

* DEMOCRACY

All people take an equal part in choosing and forming their government.

Marcus Garvey became important as the leader of the 'back-to-Africa' movement in the 1920s.

Source B

Black is beautiful.

This slogan, first used by Garvey in the 1920s, has been used many times by black Americans. It is a statement of their pride and self-respect

Many black people take great pride in their African roots. In their culture, language and sometimes their names they emphasise their African heritage. But they are also American. Americans of Italian, Jewish or Polish origin also preserve their customs but, because of their colour, black Americans have had to struggle far harder in order to be accepted even as equal human beings.

After Garvey new black leaders emerged. There have been victories but also some serious setbacks. In the section opposite you will see some of these briefly mentioned.

EVIDENCE: THE 'BACK-TO-AFRICA' MOVEMENT

1 Is Source A primary or secondary evidence?
2 Look at Source A. Why do you think the Germans dropped this message to black soldiers?
3 Do you think it would have had any effect on black soldiers?
4 What is meant by the slogan in Source B?
5 Why do you think this has been a popular slogan among black Americans?

⊃⊂ Black Americans today

- During the 1950s black people organised protests against segregation.
- In 1954 the Supreme Court said that segregation in schools was against the US Constitution.
- Still the South clung to racial discrimination. In 1963 Martin Luther King led 200,000 people on a protest march to Washington.
- In 1964 a very important civil rights act outlawed racial discrimination.

But laws cannot change people's minds. In many ways America remains a racially divided society.

In the 1950s and 1960s the song, 'We shall overcome', became the anthem of the black protest movement:

Source C

We shall overcome, we shall overcome,
We shall overcome some day.
Oh, deep in my heart I do believe,
That we shall overcome some day.

We'll walk hand in hand, we'll walk hand in hand,
We'll walk hand in hand, some day.
Oh, deep in my heart I do believe,
That we shall overcome some day.

We are not afraid, we are not afraid,
We are not afraid, today.
Oh, deep in my heart I do believe
That we shall overcome some day.

'We shall overcome'

August 1963
Thousands of peaceful civil rights marchers arrive at the Lincoln Memorial in Washington D.C. But sometimes anger and frustration over racism has resulted in riots. In 1968, following the assassination of Martin Luther King, riots occurred in more than 100 cities. Lives were lost and property was destroyed during a serious riot in Los Angeles in 1992, caused by anger over the acquittal of four white police officers who were filmed beating up a black motorist.

CHANGES

1 How have the lives of black Americans changed during the past 150 years?
2 Which changes improved their lives and which did not?
3 Have the changes brought opportunity and equal rights to black Americans?

⊃⊂ Reaching a conclusion

Now that you have studied the history of black people living in the United States of America you should be able to reach some final conclusions. In chapter one you were asked two questions:

✎ *How have black people been treated in the Americas?*
✎ *How has the experience of black people affected the course of American history?*

You were asked to form initial hypotheses to answer these questions and have since examined the evidence in the rest of the book. What are your final conclusions? You could use the diagram on the right to help you arrive at a final conclusion to the first question: Now try and draw your own diagram to help you arrive at a conclusion to the second question.

Once you have done this, does it help you to understand the behaviour of white people towards black people during the history of the USA?

- Why did many white Americans think of black people as inferior?
- Would there have been slavery if they had considered them as equal?
- Does this attitude still exist today? Why?

Conclusion

Why did black people first go to America?

Did black Americans accept their situation?

How did white southerners treat blacks after the Civil War?

What jobs did they do in America?

How have black Americans tried to improve their lives?

How were the slaves treated?

What rights did black Americans have before 1865?

How did their position compare with other Americans?

Is there any evidence that black Americans have continued to be treated unfairly?

Index

≋ Acknowledgements

The publishers would like to thank the following for permission to produce photographs:

Alabama Department of Archives and History p39 (top); Art Color Card Distributors/photo Mike Roberts p7; British Museum p5 (bottom); Colorific/photo Jim Howard p3 (top); E.T. Archive p4, p10; John Hillelson Agency p41; Hulton Deutsch Collection p34 (bottom), p36, (bottom), p45; Library of Congress p24, p38, (Syndication International) p18 (right), p35 (top), p37, p42 (both); Mansell p9 (top), p18 (left), p28 (bottom); Mary Evans p12, p16, p17 (bottom), p20 (bottom), p21 (top), p27, p29; National Geographic Society ©, Thomas Lovell Artist p32; National Portrait Gallery p17 (left); Peter Newark's American Pictures p5 (top), p8, p19 (top), p22 (bottom), p30, p31, p33 (right), p34 (top), p36 (top), p46; Nigel Smith p21 (bottom), p28 (bottom); South Carolina Division of Tourism p20 (top); Syndication International p3 (left), p15; Topham Picture Source p3 (bottom right), p14, p39 (bottom), p47; West Sussex Record Office and County Archivist/courtesy of the Governors of Dunford House p19 (bottom); Wilberforce House Museum, Hull p17 (top right); Yale University Art Gallery/Mabel Brady Garven Collection p13.

Cover photograph: National Geographic Society ©, Thomas Lovell artist

Illustrations: Tony Chance, Gerard Gibson, Fiona Powers and Martin Sanders